Contents

Open Season

Perfect Dwelling

Portrait of the Artist as an Anagram

Miscellaneous Merchandise

Directly Across from Me

Ritual

The Meaning of Need

When You Become a Body

A FIELD REMEMBERS

ANDREW MERTON

Finding the Potato

*Inside of one potato
there are mountains and rivers.*

— Shinkichi Takahashi (trans. Harold Wright)

But how to find that one potato
among all the others?
Patience, my friend.
Put your ear to the ground.
Dig where you hear thunder.

Winter Harvest

A field remembers:

every spade,
potato, fungus,
and famine
sows its own
little mound
of sorrow;

the grazing of the cows
and the plowman,

leaving.

PAUL SOHAR

The Core of Another Day

A mangled apple core
clutches the taste of the day
before yesterday.

Even its shadow
has shriveled to pale silence.
Nothing left to eat.

It's an apple skeleton,
not a spider set to pounce.
Don't have to squash it.

*

Once picked the apples were allowed to "rest"
a few days, the bruised fruit gathering flavor
before being crushed to pulp, juice expressed.
We didn't do it for money, making cider.

KRISTINE ONG MUSLIM

Pear

It was that kind
of yellow-green
mourning

which had nothing
to do with losing
something.

One wild-eye less,
it swayed—a stout
hourglass.

RUTH MOON KEMPHER

Rutabagas

blue, like old linoleum
and peaches
with fuzz and smell of bees ~
these sit on the counter, unconcerned
                as jazz
drifts over their textures, and fear
limps by, to the aspirin bottle overturned.

Sometimes vegetable, fruit ~ that's
the safest thing to be.

DM BENNINGFIELD

Bad Fruit

Melons are deceptive.
Their bruised, scarred skin
divulges nothing.

A watermelon's green rind
promises summer ripeness—
how easy to imagine deep pink pulp,
smooth texture, sweet juice.

      Insert the knife:
the melon splits clean open,
revealing no perfect pinkness
only pale and mealy flesh.

Seedless—

      a disappointment.

DEBORAH AKERS

Sunflower

noon betrays your
melancholy: grail-shaped
bloom straining its
      just-adequate
          stem

black brain
bristled with seed
      bent head
brooding the future

JOHN MCKERNAN

The Burnt Crust

Suggested iced sidewalks
Dyed with ashes

Smell of newspaper
Smoke
Sprinkled with water

The chimney said *failure*
The window mumbled *loss*
Every smoke alarm
Screamed pitch pipe woe

The rhubarb   However
Said *sugar*
Said *red*
Said *juice*   All the way
To my dry silent lips

Desert Night

I am where crevices hide.
Bluegills shatter the quiet
lake, like grief. The lake
folds itself over itself again.
The blue of my dusk hesitates.
Shadows tumble out of heat's
sheets. Wind settles the bats
with its fumbling hands. Finally
stars begin to unfold their wings.

ELIZABETH BRENNAN

I unwind the hose, send a light spray

skyward, and he is the first to see the rainbow. Bell-shaped flowers droop under the weight of even the finest drops. The unexpected shower scatters misty beads along a spider's woven silk. Green leaves at branch tips wear a polished gloss.

SARI KROSINSKY

Watercolor

it rains softly
    in Albuquerque

i can hear
    the quiet
under the motors

a woman speaks
into her cell phone
    but her voice
                disappears
    through the blue hole
in the clouds

ROBERT E. WOOD

After the Rain

water drips only
under the trees.
No one is sure
what to do
with the umbrellas.
A girl in green boots
looks for a puddle.

ERIC SCOTT SUTHERLAND

microcosm

creek beds
are cradled in
the creases of
maple leaves

DYLAN WILLOUGHBY

To An Unfallen Leaf (Northern Pin Oak)

Your withered parchment
flutters in the gust
you no longer translate the sun
but still bask in afternoon light
bright scroll you hang like
a burning book
only fire can read

Ireland/Watching Weather

Sky velvet blue behind—sheer white before—
and rain like a curtain pulled.
The furze waves its fuzzy paw.

TREY MOODY

Remembering the Original

I saw the man standing in the field at dawn.
        He was standing like a small storm.
I looked at the sky and saw the fields coming.
Waves.   The tiny storms were on their way.

CONSTANCE NORGREN

Storm

Wind out of nowhere, swirl
of papers and dust, weed-tops helpless
in the face of it.

Rain the rush of a railroad train taking a curve
and the sound way ahead.
Lightning leaving us darker.

For the lucky ones in their arks:
lift-off from land, the first slow rocking.

JANE GENTRY

Sudden Storm

O strangeness of the lake and sky
when thunder cracked out of the blue
and glistenings of the plain horsefly
trailed dark rainbows as it flew.

LYNNELL EDWARDS

The Wild and Scenic Rogue River, Oregon
(An Ideal Adventure)

Perfect storm of fun:
unspoiled, abundant, wild-
life for the photo-
graphing. What further
raft of good intentions
will you send down
the river like a rogue
wave, curled white
and snarling over the rocks?

Surf

Walk out alone:
the water giggling,
then gathering a laugh,
full of wit, wise,
but unpredictable…
on to a guffaw,
a burst of hilarity,
and finally a roaring wave,
lips full open,
head tilted back,
hands far below,
grabbing at the knees,
lecherous,
an ancient god
with serious comb-over.

J.D. SMITH

Further Shores

The sea that roars
gently in a shell
also crashes in a cup
held to the ear,
among other vessels
whose tides have only
to be taken up;
their further shores, named.

JoAnn LoVerde-Dropp

My Reward

for looking up into
the tangle of pines:

a black fist of a bird landing
steady on the storm's trick of a fallen
branch.

JO GOING

Arctic Koan

What is the sound
of summer snow
sliding suddenly
off the roof?

SHERRY CHANDLER

End of Summer

Bluster and blue sky,
gust-driven locust
leaves like drops of sun,
an oak lit neon green,
its limbs that sway in
their dance with the wind,
my rheumatic hip,
its ache as I skip
and limp in the cold.

JEANNE SHANNON

Autumn

In the night world
of owls and foxes

the cool stars come out

and the moon
is a white rose

floating

GEORGI BORISSOV

Autumn Water

Dragging rocks, trees,
torrents, flock shadows,
and having chipped away the bank,
where, where is it going?

The ice will cover you up
too, autumn water.

Only the spring will glow
black by the ice.

TOM FRAZIER

Serenity

Lotus in Chinese lagoon,
between terra and firmament,
trying to escape the one-footed crane
standing fast until first fallen snow.

JANE GENTRY

November Wind

Boanerges neighs and bucks.
Through nights, through days
he gallops on. Before him
trees bend like grass.
On his back, winter rides in.

December

On the fire escape, one
stupid petunia still blooms,
purple trumpet blowing
high notes at the sky long
after the rest of the band
has packed up
and gone home.

MARTHA GEHRINGER

January Wind/Isaiah

These trees scrub the winter sky—
scour away the grey—and I,
I bow my head like a reed.

OPEN SEASON

MATTHEW THORBURN

A Blessing

Whether it was your sister or your girlfriend
doesn't matter. We got her.
I'm writing this to say peanut butter
makes great bait. Dear mouse
behind my bookshelf, a cockroach can live
for nine days without its head
before it starves to death.
May you be so lucky.

DON BOES

Mute Zoo

My advice, like I know anything,
is to dedicate the entire day to the gallery.

Regard the clay bull from Peru
and the jade serpent from China

and the recumbent hippo
from the Middle Kingdom—

a mute and motionless zoo,
older and wiser than you.

BIANCA BARGO

Brave Fly

perched
on my
bedspread

you rub
your hands
together
like dinner's coming

no food here

I wave you
away
but you
linger

long enough
to let me
graze a wing

MARK DECARTERET

titleless

in a field
familiar
in every
way but
the birds
flying in
forced
exhalation
unlike any
I've seen
then it's winter
I'm a fountain
of trembling
in a house
w/white walls
& a lady bug
struggling
to get back
red again

REBECCA GAYLE HOWELL

How to Be an Animal:

Forget that you are an animal

Forget ancient rummaging,
pigs wild in their snouts

Forget that you ran with them,
wild between trees

wild in your cheer

NANA LAMPTON

Thoroughbred Yearling

She strikes the oak boards
with forefeet,
kicks with her hind
until the stall comes down.
I want out.

THOM WARD

Open Season

Fifty years
since it stepped
from the brush
the moose
on the wall
smiles

JEANIE THOMPSON

Prayer for the Sea Turtle

Ink shadow
like a cloud on the gulf
where your mother
sniffed the beach in moonlight,
released her brood.

When human hands lifted you,
terrible machinery
carried you,
we all held our breath—

*Find your way back
through clear waters
where you first slept*

ANDREA O'ROURKE

Lost Cow

She is thin and speaks little.
Last time she was seen at the butcher's
searching for blades of grass from her meadow.
She said the grass drooled ichor; it dribbled
on the way to the hooks, but the hooks held only
the disfigured, their mouths limp like laundry.

SAMANTHA COLE

Upon Butchering of the Hog

There is a golden time
to warn of endings
when ridge runners herd
sows from lots.
Hooks in hooves,
chain over bough.
Men of dirt drawing-up
their harvest towards the sun.

Watch and learn,
Sisters:
Struggle will ruin the meat.
The shot must be clean.

ELIZABETH OAKES

Old Cat

that proved too
expensive, tossed
out of the car
one night, left
trying to sniff
all the right turns
home. Padding

back, the dark
doesn't bother
him, a forest
is his pissing post.

E. Gail Chandler

On the Street

Each day after the pavement warms,
mama cat pads into the ditch
and retrieves her yellow kittens
from the culvert.
In the sun, they wrestle,
nestle and sleep.
Later, the bone thin cat
sniffs the trash,
the dog dish,
and one morning,
the body of her flattened baby.

CARMEN GERMAIN

Rubber Boa

When I pass the log an hour later,
the piece of wild thing is still half
in the world, half in the muscle

undulating and funneling in waves
so sating I forget I'm watching
no sun at the end of the tunnel.

PRISCILLA ATKINS

Winter Heron

Toes clasping
ice

hunching
small holes

huddle of
drab-brown

overcoat

so old
so cold

no son
no daughter

to take him
in.

RICHARD M. BERLIN

Robin in the Rafters

The viola section hears her first.
Then the conductor tilts his head
and the soloist smiles, searching
for the source of the sound overhead,
out of tune as Harpo's horn,
full throated and lusty as spring,
red breast puffed, beak aimed at the sky.

MARTHA GEHRINGER

Crows/Snow

Crows in snow—two of them—
two drops of India ink on vellum—
each one eloquent as a perfect word.

MATTHEW HAUGHTON

Starlings

Nefarious, they never seem
to travel alone—
only in packs
as if seeded by stars,
conceived the night before.

A Killdeer

His broken-wing act
is a ruse,
a game played
to spare
your shame,
for having
startled him
with the brushing
of your foot.

KATIE MANNING

Thirteen Blackbirds Looking to Do Something New

Enough of forming lines on wires, of flying in form,
     of always
wearing formal black. Enough of forming the subject
     for songs
and poems and plays. These birds tire of so much form.
Even now, the flock above me tries to pass unnoticed.

GEORGI BORISSOV

On Their Course

Flocks fly, flocks ready
for long travel,
while in fact they run, run, run
like us away from death.

In fact the days pass
on their course
and leave us only shadow
from the life of someone else.

ALBERT DEGENOVA

Tourist

pure
blue sky
wide-open two-lane
speeding past green
and brown plowed fields,
cheap cigar, loud blues music—
old
brown
horse
walks heavily
back
to
his barn
slow
ly
shaking his head

ROGER PFINGSTON

The Road Home

Winter ugly, coyote,
that bed-headed bone bag,
slinks onto the road

as I brake, gently.
Pausing, he stares up,
grinning me to a full stop.

PERFECT DWELLING

DAVID CHORLTON

Directions

Don't ask which way in the desert
every way leads straight to the sun
and don't stop once you set out to get there
every moment you lose is a drop of water
just large enough to see
your future in.

Darren Jackson

Rise and Shine

The ritual of beginning
each day razor in hand steadies the mind.
Whether we see waterspots in the glass
or the face masked in cream is a question
of focus. Steady now, it's time to begin.

JAN SEALE

The wonder is

how a tree scribbles on the sky
how the sky plagiarizes without shame
how the earth turns
page after page of grass
and we know this to be
the only handwriting on the wall

J.D. SMITH

Fragment from Zeno

Motion's largely an illusion.
Though distances narrow
By halves, then more halves, things remain apart.

While unschooled minds yield to confusion,
The bronze-tipped arrow
Only seems to pierce the roebuck's heart.

LENORE WEISS

The Collapse

so buried inside sadness
dig to remove rubble
see who walks out

daffodils say
hide in the pampas grass
with the sparrows.

DAVID SULLIVAN

Eat Your Sorrows

Burlap bag's turned back,
                reveals crisp, mounded bodies—
                            spicy grasshoppers.

Learn to eat what eats
                your crops, turn plagues of locusts
                      to delicacies.

CHRISTINA LOVIN

The Zen of Mountain Driving

Don't brake. Accelerate
through the curves. Press hard
into the steering
wheel with the outside
arm. Relax the inside
grip. Forget the road.
Lean into the arc and eye
the solid line. Unbroken,
let it carry you
around the dark mountain
and safely down.

MELISSA CARL

Lessons of the Sink

The patient spoons, their humble
gleaming.

The smallest stain's adherence
to the manner of its dish.

The water, how it gives everything
just before it takes it all back.

DIANNE APRILE

Sole Man

All day
he bows down
to his knees, greeting
feet of women, coaxing
them like cats into satin beds
of sequined flats, silk slippers
ready-to-dye. Nights at
home, before hello,
overcoat still
buttoned,
squinting at
the thermostat,
he fiddles levers
down-and-up until
we hear his furnace
stumble
shut.

KENNETH A. RICE

Daily Special

Seated alone, a prematurely gray, middle manager
is raking the unfinished pasta strands
around his plate
like tending a Japanese garden

looking for something
a bit of meat or luck or
unanswerable questions

thinking about salvation

SUCHOON MO

Shut Up!

upon the roof of a funeral home
a little bird sings

hey you
hey you
hey you you you

shut up!
a mortician says
to a corpse

RICHARD PEARSE

Starting the Workday Right

"No no no! How many times do I have to tell you—
build the body first, *then*
its coffin, or
it won't fit in!"

"Even if it's your own dad, Dad?"

"*Especially* then! Otherwise
it'll be in your way the whole workday!"

MATTHEW HAUGHTON

In the Maker's Image

Withered hand turns
a knife,
slice and peeling
an onion.
Lumps of flesh
unravel round
man and maker;
the leaves of an onion.

Violin

The violin has wings.
It is I who must use my hands.
The violin has a voice.
I am silence in the great hall.
The violin has a heart, a wild heart.
When I press its small body to me
my heart stops,
and I bow.

LEATHA KENDRICK

To Earth

End of the flight. The aisle fills with us, our
faces toward the door—crowns swirled in dark curls,
slick black swoops, coarse grizzled pepper
and salt, white tufts, silken, thinning—
time-lapse bodies sturdy, bent.
I sit, no longer
in a hurry.

GREGORY LUCE

Falling Off the Earth

is easier than you might think
sit in a small room dark or
dimly lit and avoid
the window (remember Chet Baker)
remain inside and don't answer
the telephone you will fall
away or float up.

SuzAnne C. Cole

Addiction

Termites can't digest wood.
Parasites in their bellies
assimilate the cellulose.
So who's responsible
for the craving?

MARY ANNE REESE

Midwest Apocalypse

In a stark Ohio field
on southbound 71,
a lone billboard is shouting,
"Hell is real!"

As if to illustrate, the next exchange
finds sprawling outlet malls
and traffic stalled, engulfed
in barrels orange as flames.

JEREMY DAE PADEN

Yacimiento

vein, deposit
site mined, mother lode

from yacer, to lie down, place
beside, fall ill or dead

and cimiento, foundation
root, origin, wellspring, bedrock

not to be confused
with cementerio

dump for technological waste
site where elephants go to die

burying place, forgotten stones

ARLENE L. MANDELL

Twelfth Hour

As the moon casts
long shadows through
spruce-scented woods

world leaders debate
the essence of evil
an old woman inhales
cold mountain air

a young doe in the thicket
endures her first birth.

J. KATES

Statement of a Refugee from Babel

What was most terrible was knowing
We were all saying the same thing.

DEAN CRAWFORD

Everything You Know

If everything you know is wrong,
and you know everything you know
is wrong, then everything you know
is wrong is wrong. Right?

BURTON D. WASSERMAN

At Sea

The thinking man
who dives deep
for ultimate answers
comes up naked,
races for
the fading shore.

GEORGIA WALLACE

Answers

Under the red umbrella, prayer
huddles, easing its way corner
to corner, dodging the swirling
gutters, percolating potholes,
and the city's swollen masses,
bumping one and then another,
listening in mute expectation
to the yellow amen of rain.

JOHN SIBLEY WILLIAMS

Cross, How Comfortable You Are

Cross, how comfortable you are
buried in half-sun
alongside this uncommonly long road.

ELLEN LAFLECHE

The Quietest Thing

is a woman
standing in front of
a bath-blurred mirror.
She lifts her arm.

The quietest thing
is the powder puff
slapping her wrist,
her elegant elbow.

Her first bath since the biopsy.

The quietest thing
is pink-scented talc
settling on Julia's head
like demolition dust.

CRISTINA TRAPANI-SCOTT

A Day at the Chemo Spa

We lean back in recliners
under warm blankets, drinking hot
cocoa as we are tethered to dangling
bags of liquid.

Conversation turns to weather,
though not whether there will be rain
or snow, but more specifically whether
we can hear snowflakes
as they land.

VICKIE CIMPRICH

Just After

the last flicker of angel
was gone, she wished
she were not alone, and was glad
that no one else was there.

PAUL HOSTOVSKY

Temple

The peace of God
is a piece of cake.
God's temple
is a relationship.
Any relationship.
Every relationship.
Take a look around.
The world is full of
temples. Join one.
Join them all.
Join. Join.
Joy. Joy.
The joy of God
is a piece of joinery.
It's a joint.

LAURIE CLEWETT

Note to Self

Beyond the body's pain—
an ancient well.

Behind the beating heart—
a bright expanse.

BARBARA SABOL

Happiness

The mouth
of the vase
is not calling out

for asters
for water
its cobalt glass

curves
around the notion
of flowers

a quenched stem
and window light
scattering

the blueness

MARGUERITE FLOYD

Buddha Button

Push the buddha button
There   on the navel

Press your finger into
The soft knotted flesh

Exhale slowly and wait

For tremor of earth
Split of sky

JESSICA THOMPSON

Enlightenment

sitting in silence
the opening of a door

MAUREEN TOLMAN FLANNERY

Perfect Dwelling

A place to live
 the grace
of "less is more"
 uplifted
by the holy word:
 enough,
and another place
 next door
to store the stuff

KATE ANGUS

Theosophy

Astronomers report for perhaps 2 billion years, a black hole has been singing.

DAVID BARATIER

21st Century Boy

every time a bell tone rings
on a cell phone
an angel goes berserk

JOHN MCKERNAN

The Maps of Heaven

Have been
Erased again

Some dudes
Riding Cesium algorithms
Toting sex-shooter Green-Berries

Have stored somewhere
An ocean of blood-red ink
Erased
From parchment

In an alley
Behind the burnt-out library
Black market vendors
Can fix you a speedball
Of dented Ifs & fractured Why-Nots

God

I am God
I created man
placed my hand upon
his head gently
and said You
shall have free will.
You shall not return
to me asking What
do I do next?
What do *I* do next?
What do I *do* next?

PETJA HEINRICH

Saturday Revelation #5

a real waste of time are the attempts
to smooth the edges of the wrinkled shirts
chewed up in the angry washing machine
there hadn't been soul
foam and water
in the merciless spin cycle
God is a washerwoman

NANA LAMPTON

Placement

I am a woman
on a rock,
sun on her back,
trying to feel
what the stone
has to say.

MARY ANNE REESE

The Last Joyful Mystery

I'm brushing the windshield clear
of rare Tennessee snow. A neighbor
trudges toward me, a basket on his arm.
I hope he's bringing something
Southern and homemade—biscuits,
cornbread, Christmas jam.
Perhaps a hand to clean
the car. He asks me,
"Would you like a rosary?"

NANCY FLETCHER CASSELL

The Duty of a Biscuit

Rolled out flat like dough,
pressed into a large moon
she reaches for the torn edge
waxed paper covering the kitchen counter.
Her body cut by a metal rimmed mouth
pops loose under a handle of conformity,
rising in place, she obeys heat from the oven.

PORTRAIT OF THE ARTIST AS AN ANAGRAM

ALEX CIGALE

Portrait of the Artist as an Anagram

A caldera of intimation, a cinder,
a bright relic in a penny arcade,
a candela, a radiant dalliance,
a break in the calendar, when I cried,
a grained reading. I lingered, an Inca
reclined on an edge, a dicier side receding.

A. H. JERRIOD AVANT

A Poet's Night

Our nights come gifting
us with burning stars,

sifted by the con-
tours this language carves.

We, gang of pushers
of verbal flowers
awaiting orders

from our stars to bury
us in showers.

Our suns rise all night,
ripping packaging off
talents coming wrapped
inside life.

FREDERICK SMOCK

To Li Po

Here's to Li Po,
drinking wine on the riverbank
under willows, cheering
the paper boats floating along
toward the capitol,

and look, now there is
a new constellation in the east,
Li Po Drinking Wine,
lifting a goblet of stars
to his black black lips....

TOM C. HUNLEY

World's Shortest Pantoum

To break the record
for the world's shortest pantoum
you must make every word
feel like the prettiest girl in the room.

For the world's shortest pantoum
you must make almost every word
in every stanza (Italian for *room*),
repeat like a broken record.

ANDREW MERTON

Subjunctive

The timid grammarian,
unable to approach the object
of his unspoken proposition,
is destined to dwell forever
alone in the woulds.

LARRY W. MOORE

Grammar

Ever and endless English major,
correcting me one last time
on the use of *further* and *farther*.
Which *are* you, now?

Feel

Said fill. It's heavier
That way. The chin sags
With its weight
Like a roof droops
Under pooled rain. Feel
Slices the mouth into smile.
Fill's dull, sadder than that.
You couldn't split wood
With a word like fill.
Fill's a flat basketball
Floating down the river
Of words.

KRISTINE ONG MUSLIM

And

Not yet a poem. This one
is a being, a conscious slip

which tries to make its point
then fails. It is part of

a larger hunger with
hands too big to become

a river, with a grip too un-
steady to hand its water back.

KEITH S. WILSON

Fishing

A book must be the axe for the frozen sea inside us.
                                        —Kafka

Imagine
the word that upsets
the velocity of a day.

The heavy salt
charge.

Imagine
knowing that word.

Imagine
catching it.

JEREMY DAE PADEN

I Wrote This Note

after *William Carlos Williams*

to say,
if my last poem
caused you any pain
forgive me:

not every truth
I tell is mine,
not every truth
I tell is true,

sometimes
I write
even when
the muses
aren't speaking.

JEN KOHAN

Revision

Put the firework back together
Unring the bell
Gather up the shreds of scream
Push it back behind your tongue

A second look
Is not the first
And you've changed
Since then.

MISCELLANEOUS MERCHANDISE

PRAIRIE L. MARKUSSEN

Even Means

"I don't even know what that means."
Don't even. I know that means. Even
I. Know means know. Don't! What
means even? What means don't? I
know even means even. I even know
that. What? Know means don't. Even
even even! Don't. I know that.

Cheeseburgers

There's a legend about Richard Brautigan
buying a house in Marin County.
He replaces everything in the house with books,
everything:

> plumbing,
> heating/cooling,
> electrical wiring,
> appliances,
> and furniture.

I know a guy who knows the guy who buys the house
from Brautigan. He replaces all the books
with cheeseburgers.

ROGER CRAIK

Conference Going

In the room the women come and go
Talking of Maya Angelou.

PAUL HOSTOVSKY

Nose

Hers the only
red leaf in winter
that never fell.

DAVID BARATIER

Trained Cartoonist

You won't suddenly turn around
and find a puddle of piss
drawn in the corner

DAVID PARK MUSELLA

Misrepresentations: Skipping Stones

It took that rock
thousands of years
to reach the shore,
and
      you
          just
              threw
                    it
                        back.

NICHOLAS LIU

Tercet

the starfish-sprawl
of minor cities, each approaching cliché
from its own appropriate distance

RICHARD LEVINE

Puddle

The sun shines
between two
parked cars

a 747
disappears
into the pavement

JENNIFER LITT

Jared Loughlin's Glock

The Safeway?
Not my way
nor my ammunition clip's,
I'm semi-automatic, slick,
a deadly *click, click, click.*
I'm on the hunt.
I'm Jared's glock
Tick tock
Tick tock
The sound of your life running out…

CAROL LEVIN

History's Juju

In 1944 Edward Teller pressed the button
on the Trinity bomb knowing
the atmosphere could

catch fire
The fire could circle and end the earth.
Teller pressed it
and waited.

NANCY FIERSTIEN

Independence

This land is mine,
this land mine's mine—
I found it in the street.

How lucky for me!
I continue to be.

I hobble, wobble,
stand
on my own new feet.

NANCY FIERSTIEN

The Paraplegic's Paradox

My knees buckle;
a fly walks by
on legs
no thicker than my hair.

How it pains me
to compare
the way I sit,
the way I stare.

LIBBY FALK JONES

Like a Dog a Weasel, I Chase Sleep

finally I tackle her

grip her tail
in my mouth

from side to side
thrash her

CHRISTINE STREVINSKY

My Elephant

is a happy beast;
pansies and petunias
garland his ears,
butterflies perch
on his back.

He munches silver grass
and gossips with the zebras
who live in the next frame
right above my bed.

GABRIELE A. ROLLÉ

Air Raid

The attic next door looks full of smoke.
Someone cradles a suitcase and steps
out the window. Of course he falls.

DAVID CHORLTON

The Discovery of Father Francisco Javier Saeta's Remains

There was little to collect.
Some bones and dried blood.
Many arrows.
The soldiers worked respectfully
as they scraped a long scream
from the whitewashed wall.

-ING

I. Breaking and Entering

House
Room
Person
Heart
Story
Plot
Fights
Sex
Fights
Sex
Fights
Silence
Strangers

BRETT EUGENE RALPH

January

Who's it gonna be
dragging that dead Xmas tree
deep into the woods

CHARLIE HUGHES

Poem Found
on Nicholasville Road

Guaranteed
Used Tires

Buy One
Get One.

STACI R. SCHOENFELD

On the Way Home from Lexington to Frankfort via Leestown Road

A sign proclaims
justice for sale.

There are four white
open mailboxes, waiting.

A turtle, the size
of a dinner plate, is crossing.

Buffalos, alpacas,
and cows are grazing.

At the pumpkin patch,
someone's selling strawberries.

MARK DECARTERET

fable

I've had
no luck
finding
the forest
I was supposed
to have been
lost in
forever
and ever

DAVID PARK MUSELLA

Beige

It's not just a color;
it's a way of life.

DAVID PARK MUSELLA

*

Dreams don't end.
They go on without you.

KATE ANGUS

Time Passing

A damp woolen coat hung over the sharp hook of what you remember.

ADAM DAY

Badger Eats

Here is Badger in a small room,
knotted nipples among a bed
of gray hair, the mud-caked
knuckles, gristle-mouthed
with a vole carcass, the moss-scummed
walls, the cellar door's rusted
padlock, the wheeze of pulleys
outside, geese barking and dark
water under a shelf of snow.

RICHARD SCHIFFMAN

Flamingo

Pretty flamingo
in a pink spandex pants suit
perched upon a twiggy leg,
cradling a cell phone
in Grand Central.
As commuters pour
like Mongol hordes,
she tucks her head
beneath a wing
for better reception.

SHERI L. WRIGHT

Shedding

A lusty-lipped woman
can speak in ways
that strip off
our nine-to-five selves,
our neatly-arranged days
fit and creased
without an inch to spare
for alterations.
She will have us
fling it all away,
strewn behind
as we follow
the curve
of her smile.

Apology

The beautiful woman
wears the same dress,
twice.

STACI R. SCHOENFELD

Miscellaneous Merchandise

a found poem

Two prom dresses.
One long,
one short.
Must see.

ROB MCLENNAN

Sum

(everything)

)else(

DIRECTLY ACROSS FROM ME

A. H. JERRIOD AVANT

Control

I. See how that works?
I.
Not
him her he or she
or you or y'all or them
no they, nor it.
Just
me,
I.
Then, just watch us.

BIANCA SPRIGGS

This Is Not a Self-Portrait

My hand is not steady enough
to hold my reflection straight.
Here, in a cracked compact
mirror: one floating
near-sighted eye,
briar thatch of hair,
an overgrown nostril,
a wayward tooth,
eyebrows crawling
to meet—

    rumors

of what lies unsettled
beneath the skin.

House Guests

Our future selves arrive
like old friends
crashing for the night,
but who never leave:
their toothbrushes becoming
fixtures & the milk emptying
from jug to their lips, slugtrailing
their chins. What kind of hosts
would we be if we didn't
raise our hands,
dab our faces clean?

PEGGY LANDSMAN

Silhouette

If you weren't you and I weren't I
We two could live as one

But I *am* I
You are stuck

Standing in old friends' doorways
Wearing unflattering shoes.

CONNIE ABSTON

Friend
for J and H

Sunshine is a verb,
  as is divine,
which I do
  absorbing you.

JAY McCoy

Selfish

You & I were inseparable
as children, grew

apart as adults, but remained
close in spirit, despite

the distance. Seven years after—
your mother cannot see

me without crying, so I stopped
going to visit her last year

for my own good.

KATHLEEN GERARD

The Art of Giving

You were my favorite—
Aran Irish wool
eight buttons—
lent to a friend
who was boarding a chilly plane
after a weekend visit.
She promised to ship you back.
That was two years ago.
I never ask for you
but I know exactly where you are.

GERALD FLEMING

To a Friend with Whom I Had a Falling Out

May your waters run
clear.
May they run
clean.
May they run
on the other side
of the divide
from mine,
many miles
between.

PAUL SOHAR

This Wine of Mine

This wine is no good—
I know it and they know it.

That's why they pour it
in my glass

not even suspecting
that someday

I'll throw it up in their faces
and then this wine will be good.

Very good.
I can taste it already.

DAVID BARATIER

Biography

If there's nothing here
it's probably mine
so take it with you
when you go walking

this morning.
I ain't remembered yet

how willing I am to replace
this piece of past, how
three shots from a .22
can surround the heart.

ANDREI GURUIANU

Weather Depending

When eternity began its incessant barking
I slipped on the muzzle, took it for a walk.

What a beautiful specimen, said one.
What sunken jowls, said another.

We pulled in different directions,
arms straining in their sockets.

We looked like old chums.
The knife respectfully out of sight.

Tina Andry

considerate

i cut myself shaving
thought i would save
you the trouble.

DAVID PARK MUSELLA

Mea Culpa

The person I meant to become
would more easily forgive me
for not becoming that person
than the person I have become
ever could.

LIBBY FALK JONES

Fe/Male

Today at the plumbing store counter
I put on my lipstick.

Around me, men
with heavy jowls,
hairy arms,
speak of plastic parts
and female ends.

In the circle of my compact
my lips glare
an o.

At Jane's Dojo

She doesn't need
                    the black belt
to set her off. The whites,
                    yellows,
                    browns and
                    reds
show themselves
in their clumsy
                    movements, cubes all
                    elbow and knee
                    rolling hard-angled
over the mats. When she throws me
    she is a ripple
in still water and I
                    am flying.

MARILYN KALLET

Thirst

I long for what disturbs
her, for the splinter
she complains of,
I'm jealous of what
has gotten into her today.

Nothing strikes close.

CAROLINE A. LEBLANC

Fire Fights

He doesn't say much about them, only,
"No one tells you that everything
starts to move in slow motion,
even the flash that turns
your buddy into mist."

Tom C. Hunley

Having Banished the Musicians

they headed for battle—

the trumpeter blew in his prison cell;
the drummer kept time.

A sketch artist on the front lines
caricatured the enemy general;

an avant garde poet recited verses
that underscored the senselessness

of what they were about to do.

ANDREI GURUIANU

Arrivals

The clock in the plaza
showed the wrong time,
which was just right for somewhere else.

And why were you so surprised
that at that hour
we simply did not exist?

It wasn't our turn yet.
The clock had three other faces—
each for a different hour of need.

At the Terminal

at dusk, I wait, I've waited, I will wait.
I'm doing the dance of a man at an airport,
pacing on the far side of the gate.
Air has beaks and beady eyes.
I'm not up for the leap across open sky.
Plummet. Free-fall. That's my take.

ZACK ROGOW

At the Gate

stranger sitting directly
across from me
waiting for the same plane
what life
are you returning to

WANDA FRIES

At the Pub

He slides his arm
around her shoulders
winks and mouths *barfly*
over the top of her hair
as if she is the only one here
snugged up to the edge
willing to lap up death
from a stranger

LISA ZIMMERMAN

On the Kindness of Strangers

To the man in the white pickup truck driving past
me in my little Honda on Highway 34,
who pointed out his window
that my silk skirt was trapped in my car door
and flapping its floral sail above the asphalt—
thank you.

COLLEEN S. HARRIS

Young Veteran

He met his wife in
a fender-bender, says
he could tell she had
a lovely behind and
wanted to meet her.
He does not say
he missed the brake
because of his surprise
at a stranger's eyes
looking back from
the rearview mirror.

RITUAL

ELIZABETH IANNACI

His First Cry

is small and fierce. Suddenly,
I can no longer be trusted
with secrets. Tell me nothing
vital: I would give it up
in an instant. Now, there is
something in life
worth ransom.

ELIZABETH BURK

Discovering the Sky

Tiny blue sneakers
on spiky green grass
head tilted skywards
my son balances upright
slowly swivels his gaze
surveys cotton clouds suspended
in vast azure. Face lit
like a jack-o'-lantern
fists clenched for balance, he sways,
takes his first step away
into this great awe-ful world.

MARIAN VEVERKA

A Grandchild Turns Two

You sat on the sand and laughed
Each time a wave curled over
Your feet. All the people on
The beach laughed with you.
How thoughtful of you and
Lake Erie to entertain a
Group of people who had
Grown weary of the world.

SARAH BUSSE

daughter I did see

flapwing, one day you
    I swear chair to couch
        flew

little flitter toe-
    walker red-haired dragon
        fly

ANTHONY FRAME

This Small Poem

freezes a dog mid-bark, his jaw widened
to a vacuum. Two six-year-old boys watch

ants build homes. Their father, a sweating cloud,
shadows them with his bulk and briefcase.

BOBBI BURNS

October Addison

six years old and
covered in pumpkin

hers is a first-grade
jack-o'-lantern grin
a flame flickers
in that happy gap

a tiny beacon
on a dark fall night

NORMAN MINNICK

Painting

for Terrance Hayes

By the time I got around to it
there was a hole in the canvas
from my children peeking
into the next world.

WENDY VARDAMAN

Mother Contemplates the Assumption

It's all any mother wants
for her first-born—
his ascension,

then a hand
into heaven.

CHUNGYEN CHANG

When My Mother Broke Her Wrist

I told her to leave him. She said
he was a good man—
most of the time.

She told him to leave. He said
he was a good man—
most of the time.

JENNIFER BECKETT

Single-Parent Math

She said, *We have*
Kiddie Bacon. It's specially made
just for kids; you're so lucky

and I gobbled up the story,
unquestioning or unaware

how two pieces in the fridge
turned into four for me and a friend

and where was Mom's plate?

ELIZABETH BECK

Incest Survivor

the worst part of being
an old whore
by the age of eight
is how jaded you feel
when you blow
out twelve candles.

GEORGE ELLA LYON

Gift

So much my mother
forbade me to say.

What could I do but sing?

LISA KANG

Adumbratim: Shadowed Things

Mother, when the moon passes
Dark before the sun like an age

Spot on the face of heaven
The corona's sudden brilliance

Unfurls in waves to light
The blighted sky like your smile

On the days you remember
Who I am.

GEORGE ELLA LYON

Ritual

With my grandmother's scissors
I cut the stems of wildflowers
to fit the smaller vase.
Yes! We are all
happier
now.

PHILIP DACEY

Thumb

The odd, friendless boy raised by four aunts.

MARK RUSSELL BROWN

The Day I Came Out to Aunt Wib

I unraveled on her
sewing room couch

and my seams popped—
"I'm gay" spilled out.

"No, you're not," she fumbled
to restuff and patch me,

and we resumed cutting
patterns for Barbie doll hats.

ANDREW MERTON

Third Cousin, Twice Removed

The first time it took a restraining order.
The second time it was too late.

ELIZABETH IANNACI

My Father, on War:

If you had my eyes
you still wouldn't
see things my way.

MARIN BODAKOV

(I dream that I'm dancing)

two men,
elderly father and elderly son
dance a tango—
and the father drags the son towards the sidewalk
in mute music

Two Men in a Bathroom

When the son must
shave his father
since the old man's hand
began to shake too much
to draw the straight razor
smoothly through the lather
on his cancerous jaw,

his hand trembles too.
Oh! they both cry out.

BARRY GEORGE

Ritual

After dinner every night,
my father, standing by the sink,
would fill a glass with water,
place one fisted hand behind his hip,
throw back his head, and drink
until it was empty.

JULIE BROOKS BARBOUR

Honeybee, Woman

Even the young workers
care for the youngest.
We forage, we dance.
We cook, we clean.
We guard the family.
All in a day's work.

PETER RAMOS

King Size Bed

Plump and wide, gigantic
sheet cake with vanilla frosting!

Big enough for dad
and mom, even the kids.

We'd come between them. We'd sleep
all of us dreaming, drifting

apart. One night my brother and I
opened our eyes and split. At dawn

our parents awoke, suddenly
strangers.

NICHOLAS RIPATRAZONE

Magic

The man on stage rolled a quarter
across his knuckles, silver climbing skin
before disappearing into jacket sleeve
but the real trick
sat in the third row:
my mother,
holding hands with another man
and by the end of the show his palm
smothered hers, and she
was gone.

KENNETH POBO

Meadow Rue

I think of my grandmother's white hair
when I see how full it is,

charming, nothing else quite
so eye-catching,

and no way to stop
August from coming.

LORI A. MAY

Hindsight

I'm suspicious of the salt jar
and how it was once mistaken
for sugar:
my mother's guests
amused as she served
bitter cream pie.

THE MEANING OF NEED

ROB MCLENNAN

The End of Innocence

I am going to invent a new month.

we say things such as 'yes' & 'I want you.'
we use proper names.

this is a love poem.

ALBERT DEGENOVA

No Small Typo

You demand, you command
with the drop of a comma
at the close of a letter
no small typo
this slip of the finger
love me
without proper punctuation
is more than flirtation
more than fire to a moth
more like
the cannibal's dinner bell.

MARY E. O'DELL

No Sapling Love

We are two old oaks
rooted each in our patch of earth
leaning together
crowns near enough
for the sparrows to flit
through our mingled branches.

SHEILA BUCY POTTER

Visit to a Winery

The older plants have fewer grapes,
But make a sweeter wine.
I thought, how very like my heart,
That knotted, twisted vine.

J. KATES

The Wrist

Bones rise
under the skin
like sharks
in shallow water.
Here the skeleton
shows itself—
so wise uncles
prophesy
the grown size
of small children
by the span
of their wrists—
and so
I kiss the hollow
of your own,
making love
to the bone.

RICHARD LEVINE

Lust

Stars are furnaces, did they
tell you, set against cold,

black sky, burning like a
woman's thighs in thoughts

the baker kneads into
loaves before sunrise.

KAREN RIGBY

Bread

Pitas swell, parachutes
in their ovens. On holidays, wreaths

braided with raisins.
I like a simple loaf best.

No olives greasy as pennies,
dry crust flaking

in my hands, torn magnolias
clean as bodies

after love. The first time a man
fed me bread, pockets of air

were shutters opening.

BOBBI DAWN RIGHTMYER

Choices

Rainy, not sunny
Yellow daises, not red roses
Family night, not late nights out
Rocks, not jewelry
Books, not television
Freshly mown grass, not perfume
Moonlight, not sunshine
Late nights, not early mornings
Fall, not winter
Hugs, not hits
Kisses, not screams
You and me, not me without you

ANTHONY FRAME

Furlough Days

As my wife readies for work, I'm still
wearing sleep pants. She dries her hair

as I prepare her toast, watching the bees
outside dance on our Rose of Sharon bush.

Yes, love, I burnt the toast. I was dreaming
of our wings, our striped backs, our pollen.

Love Me

Green me,
watermelon me,
honeydew me,

of honey
and of dew
make me,

peel me,
slice me,
eat me,

and throw my rind
into the sky,
marked by your teeth,

and spit my seeds
over the rooftops:
brilliant stars.

KAREN GEORGE

Rapture

Leaves brush the car roof in a turnaround
tucked under a catalpa. I follow you
single file on a path the forest is reclaiming.
The woods hum around me like a second skin.

Automat Luv

push a button
now drop me a slice

nice

now warm it up
serve it hot

every drop
every drop

KATE ANGUS

Longing

Ever since you touched my wrist, the world is a room full of apples.

ANTHONY FIFE

The Gift

I wanted a gift for you, but
didn't know how
          thought of your dark hair, how it
always needed ribbons   Bought
a pair of scissors for the giving
tied with a blue bow

JAMES VINCENT

A Nail

The last thing I need
to hang
this picture of you

TOM C. HUNLEY

Understanding Love

is like understanding a drum solo.
Better to let it shake your bones.
Or understanding how they score
Olympic skaters. Better to hold your breath
as he holds her hand, her head inches from
the ice, cheering their routine
whether or not they stumble.

GREG BACHAR

Rain

Rain fell
on the roof
of my car.

Fingers drummed
on the hood
of my future
wreck.

I leaned over
for a first kiss.

Tap Tap,
the rain said,
more is on its way.

RICHARD TAYLOR

Romances

Too many evolve like the flightless cormorant
off the coast of Chile that never achieves flight

but skims across the water, its wings beating
against surfaces of air and water in audible

flappings, the onlooker's eye recording
little spits and frenzies where it touches.

CHRISTOPHER MCCURRY

Two in a Twin Bed

Being tangled together
is only uncomfortable
until you stop squirming.

Then you're part of one another
like a body caught
in a barbed-wire fence.

KAREN STROMBERG

Lighthouse

Realizing
this impenetrable
silence
is your response,
I begin making my way up
the steep circular steps
of yet another
apology.

MARK DECARTERET

cycle

she'll wheel (within wheel)
while he'll wheel (within wheel) while
we'll wish them all well

JANE GENTRY

Why Marriage Works

Nothing you want from me.
Nothing I need from you.
Satisfied now
with what we have given,
what we have gotten,
we lie sleep-heavy,
notched to the other,
the primordial struggle
forgotten.

ROSEMERRY WAHTOLA TROMMER

*

Because I have come undone before
I bring you these yellow petals.
They will not fashion into a flower again,

but see how sweetly the wind gathers them
and releases, releases, releases.

JOY GAINES-FRIEDLER

Getting Rid of the Spider

He said, I can't cure her
missing childhood. Can't be
her astounded father, replace her
unmothering. I can only crack open
this beer, listen to the crickets,
hope their calls don't sound
too much like loneliness to her.

ANDREW MERTON

Keys

Near dawn
in a strange part of town

I lock myself out of my car.
Through the window I see

my keys in the ignition,
my phone on the seat,

and, on the floor,
a note from a woman:

What has happened?
I feel a terrible distance between us.

ADA JILL SCHNEIDER

Elasticity

I am your bungee woman
head over heels,
bounce to rebound,
always attached,
free-fall and all.
Between us
a certain elasticity,
a bouncing back,
give and take,
pliant pitch,
resilient catch,
back and forth
at your touch
like a swinging
weight on a string.
I always come back.

BRETT EUGENE RALPH

Elegy for Lorri

One time we got high
together in the bathroom stall
of a bar. There was trouble
keeping it lit, so when I'd had my hit,
I hurried, holding it up
to where your lips were.

JOEL LONG

Desert Matin

The sparrow slips among
pear blossoms. The cow is lowing
behind the fences. I am without
you this morning, but in this blue,
in this growing warmth, there is
no sound that is not your name.
There is no light
where your name is
no longer written.

RUTH FOLEY

Moving

You say home is made,
created like a garden.
I grew nothing here.

Things we'll never need:
orphaned sock, old-man sweater.
I pack your letters.

Liquor store boxes
full of poetry and song—
we both drink to that.

In the compost bin
forsythia forced itself
to farewell yellow.

AIMEE MACKOVIC

Note to an Ex

Our adopted philodendron
is taking over

the window sill, a survivor
thriving in August

heat, taking the direct sun
like a champ. I watch

each new leaf sprout
like a little waxy bullet.

Still, I water it daily,
like clockwork.

CHOCOLATE WATERS

I Used To

make love.
Now I
make coffee.

DARIEL SUAREZ

Match-Made

She liked to tease the sun
and walk in silence.
I was a field of dry leaves.

JERRY RATCH

When I'm Not Here

She'll get a dog
a Weimaraner
I know

She'll call him Alfie
after her first
two dogs

He'll try to get up
on the bed
She'll say, Alfie, no, no

But in the night
she will let him
so as not to be lonely

JESSE MANLEY

Today I Threw Out Your Toothbrush

Now only two things of yours remain:

the stain on my sheets from that time
neither of us could wait

and your running shoes,
which maybe you'll return for
because they still have some miles left in them.

ROSEMERRY WAHTOLA TROMMER

All in an Effort to Not Think About

Rise,
stretch,
bathe,
dry,
crack,
whisk,
sizzle,
fry,
then
drive
dash
do
cross
the
list
through
hike
teach
call
reach
meet
eat
brush
rush
slide
hide
cry
lie.

NICHOLAS LIU

Youtube on Love

Sad to be the turtle. How much sadder to be the shoe.

AMY ASH

Absence

It is dusk, and I am trying
to decipher the meaning of purple.

All I can come up with is the meaning
of need. My reflection in the window,
translucent, frail.

The Rorschach of oil spill
just visible in the faint porch light
where your car belongs.

KATHLEEN HENSLEY

Short Days

Longing is gristled
Frigid nights with three blankets
Tea too far from bed
Cigarettes not worth smoking
Limbs coiled to save from despair

NETTIE FARRIS

Dear M

John
Mayer
asked

me
to
be

his
Valen-
tine!—

so
don't
worry

about
forgetting
me. love n

IVAN LANDZHEV

Song of Myself

Women often are curious
and ask, "Who have you written
that poem about?"
I think a bit,
then always answer, "Me."

JOANIE DIMARTINO

Divorcing the Strong Man

the never retrieved
beads he

cleaved from her neck

clattered to the floor
        scattered

beneath the chest
of drawers

OLIVIA V. AMBROGIO

#1 of Philippa's Questions

Let's imagine
I fall into disuse
like that one old pair
of rusty shears
no one bothers with anymore.
& let's say you come along
in need of pruning.

(how long, do you think,
old blades take to sharpen?)

WHEN YOU BECOME A BODY

KEITH S. WILSON

Leaving the Garden

Your thoughts will burden
into the body of a flower
pressed in a book,
fragile and beautiful as snow.
So cold. A weathered bloom
unable to open for anyone.

ALAN ELYSHEVITZ

Brevity

I was born
yesterday
and die
tomorrow.
Today
I mourn my own
outcome
and take my tea
with the lemon of
inevitability.
Honey
finds its greatest
absence
in the body of
a bee.

GAIL CARSON LEVINE

This Is Just to Say

after *William Carlos Williams*

that today
I will
lose
my life

which
you hoped
would last
a lot longer

Forgive me
I miss your father
too much
to get well

SHERRY CHANDLER

No More

Mother curls, hands clawed.

She is warm, but shrunk,
dry as a thing
unearthed. We

hang on each chest fall,

not sad yet, but holding
each our own breath.

Then she is still.

JOE PEACOCK

The Dying

"How come you're taking Daddy's clothes?"

Mom covers her eyes and weeps.

Pulling me into the hallway,
my brother whispers in a quiet voice,
a voice strong and quiet
for his twelve years,
he whispers,
shhh-h-h,
he whispers:

Just
keep
your
goddamn
mouth
shut.

And I did that.

MARIANNE WORTHINGTON

Thanksgiving Eve

My mother sleeps in my bed,
my father sleeps
in a ground starting to freeze.
I wake in a moon-lit room
not meant for sleeping.
What else to do but let go
of his wheelchair and inhalers,
his starched pajamas pressed
and resting in his cherry dresser?

CHARLOTTE MANDEL

Seven-Day Candle

Choosing sin over chance of fire
I blow out the flame burning in a glass cylinder
on my fifth day of mourning.

Hardening wax coats
the blue sixpointed star
above the letters In Memoriam.

Blackened wick quivers in a pool of melt.
Have I hobbled my father's soul?

MARIN BODAKOV

(I dream that I cover the grave with wet blankets)

my father's bodies—
no irresponsible copies, just originals,
many bodies of the same old man—

stretching everywhere around my home,
face down

JOHN SIBLEY WILLIAMS

Psalm Two

I don't need a chin to rest upon this clenched fist.

I don't need fists to blindly pound the earth, or sky.

I don't need earth to tell where this body has been
or sky to remember where it has not.

Sunflower River Road

This road bends around
cane swamps, raises

a thick dust to hide
the end of day. I am sorry

for my silence, ashamed
that I have words

for this road and none
for your dying. I can even

hear the green cries
of cypress trees.

FRANCIS KRUG

Unci

In a picture,
she has on a buckskin dress.
The one she was going to wear
to my graduation.

SONJA DE VRIES

Michael's Mother

leans down
to kiss
his forehead,
smooth his
hair, and adjust
the toy dog
under her son's arm,
before
the funeral
director closes
the coffin.

AMY WATKINS

Anniversary of the Death of a Child

My mother's porch swing.
Orange blossoms pulled by dry wind—
the smell of April.

KAREN MCPHERSON

After

a postscript to a life he says
in exile
from his phantom city

in this drowsy town of trees
there's too much
sky his days and nights
keep changing places

she's gone a year five months
today he writes
nothing since
each thought
contains its own
unanswer

SARI KROSINSKY

Dead Letters

People die, and the mail
keeps coming. I know this
because the video catalogues
come back to me. The mourners
scrawl "DECEASED" in block letters
across Keira Knightley's cheek.
I update the database,
delete the dead.

PIOTR GWIAZDA

The Dead

play cards in Trenton
at a picnic table

under raised hatch doors
of two Dodge Caravans

in the wet empty parking lot
illumined by candles

over unfinished dinner.

PEGGY LANDSMAN

Nicolae and Elena Ceausescu

Looking at a newspaper photograph of their execution—12/25/89

in death
they do not look
like tyrants.

slumped against
that wall,
eyes closed

no more evil
than any two
elderly shoppers

caught
at day's end—
wiped out.

ALEX CIGALE

*

Separate sections in Mexican cemeteries
for recently deceased and long departed,
the dead remembered and the truly dead.

FRANCIS KRUG

Closure

The fresh dirt
from Grandmother's grave
had cattle tracks.

ALLISON THORPE

Beauty

After Georgia O'Keefe's *Horse's Skull with White Rose*

Absent of flesh
How free the spirit
Wind humming bone
Angular instrument
A harmony of socket, nostril, tooth
Bleached velvet mantra
Proudly rivaling
The refrain of bloom

ELIZABETH OAKES

Being Born, Then Dying

When you become a body,
it tightens around
you with a sound like
insects in a haiku.

Then, this body loosens
like jeans you've worn
three times, and you will
slip out of it with no
more thought than that.

THOM WARD

What Do You Want When You Leave?

The dance of rain on dirt. Pears
in a glass bowl. Children on swings.
Three flowers, one for you, my shadow
and the guest who has yet to arrive.
The rusted wheelbarrow at the edge
of the woods. This and that and these.

Authors

Connie Abston is a fourth generation Memphian who has lived in England and is currently at work on a series of word poems.

A lifelong Westerner, **Deborah Akers** was born in Colorado. She now lives in Portland, Oregon. Her first chapbook, *backward pilgrim*, is upcoming from I-Beam Books.

Olivia V. Ambrogio's work has appeared in over 20 literary journals. Her blog, beastsinapopulouscity.blogspot.com, offers photos and observations of zoo-/wildlife.

Tina Andry, a made-from-scratch poet originally from New Orleans, now lives in Lexington, Kentucky with her two children.

Kate Angus's work has appeared in places like *Barrow Street*, *Subtropics*, *Third Coast* and *Best New Poets 2010*. She is an editor at Augury Books.

Dianne Aprile teaches creative non-fiction on the faculty of Spalding University's MFA in Writing program. She lives in Seattle where she's at work on a memoir.

Amy Ash is a Pushcart nominee and an Academy of American Poets prize recipient. She has poems forthcoming in *Prairie Schooner* and *Slipstream*.

Priscilla Atkins lives near the intersection of two lakes, in a town where Main Street never ices over in winter.

A. H. Jerriod Avant was raised in Longtown, Mississippi. A Jackson State University alumnus, he's currently a 2nd-year MFA (poetry) student at Spalding University in Louisville, Kentucky.

Greg Bachar lives in Seattle. His writing has appeared previously in *Conduit*, *Rain Taxi*, *Dislocate*, *Indiana Review*, and *Quick Fiction*.

David Baratier has seven chapbooks, mild superpowers, and a book of creative non-fiction *In It What's in It* from Spuyten Duyvil. He is the editor of Pavement Saw Press.

Julie Brooks Barbour's poems have appeared or are forthcoming in *UCity Review, Kestrel, Waccamaw,* and *Migrations: Poetry and Prose for Life's Transitions.*

Bianca Bargo is a southeastern Kentuckian, 2009 Farquhar Poetry Award Winner, and University of Kentucky graduate. She currently lives in Lexington, Kentucky where she is inspired daily.

Elizabeth Beck is a writer, artist, and teacher. She and her family live on a pond in Lexington, Kentucky.

Jennifer Beckett lives in Georgetown, Kentucky. She graduated from Georgetown College and teaches English and French. She has been published in *The Heartland Review.*

DM Benningfield's work has appeared on Lexington's Accents radio program, in *Southern Women's Review,* and *Aurora.* She's currently writing her first novel and chapbook.

Carol Berg's poems are forthcoming or in *Mslexia, Fifth Wednesday Journal, qarrtsiluni,* and elsewhere. Her website is located at carolbergpoetry.com/wordpress/.

Richard M. Berlin is a poet and physician who lives in a rural town in the Berkshire hills of western Massachusetts.

Marin Bodakov is the author of several books of poetry, most recently *Naïve Art.*

Don Boes appears in the anthology *What Comes Down To Us: 25 Contemporary Kentucky Poets* (University Press of Kentucky). He teaches at Bluegrass Community and Technical College.

Georgi Borissov is the author of a number of books of poetry in Bulgarian. He lives in Sofia and Paris.

Elizabeth Brennan lives in Sonoma County, California. She is author of the chapbook *Sewing Her Hand to the Face of the Fleeting* (Quale Press).

Mark Russell Brown, from Louisville, Kentucky, received his MFA from Spalding University. His work can be found in *The Louisville Review*, *BloodLotus,* and *Bloom.*

Elizabeth Burk is a psychologist currently dividing her time between a practice in New York and a husband in southwest Louisiana. Her poetry appears in various journals.

Bobbi Burns is a native of Topeka, Kansas. She currently lives in Lexington, Kentucky, where her love for writing has flourished.

Sarah Busse is co-editor of *Verse Wisconsin* (versewisconsin.org) and author of *Quiver* (Red Dragonfly Press) and *Given These Magics* (Finishing Line Press). She lives in Madison, Wisconsin.

Melissa Carl has published her poems in a variety of venues, both print and online. She teaches history and resides in Pennsylvania and North Carolina.

Nancy Fletcher Cassell's poems have appeared in *Still: The Journal* and *Water-Stone Review.* Cassell received a Legacies Award from the Carnegie Center for Literacy and Learning (2007).

E. Gail Chandler retired from Kentucky Corrections. She's written two books: *Sunflowers on Market Street* (nonfiction) and *Where the Red Road Meets the Sky* (poetry).

Sherry Chandler's first full-length collection of poetry, *Weaving a New Eden*, has recently been released by Wind Publications.

Chungyen Chang is a radical Asian American male Feminist at Berea College. He believes in writing as a solution to silence the path to healing.

David Chorlton recently had a poem included in the British Museum anthology *BIRDS*, and won the Slipstream Chapbook Contest with *From the Age of Miracles*.

Alex Cigale's translations of Russian Silver Age miniature and contemporary minimalist poems are online at *Offcourse* (albany.edu, issue 41) and *Alba* (Ravenna Press, issue 21), respectively.

Pretty Mother's Home: A Shakeress Daybook (Broadstone Books, 2007) is **Vickie Cimprich**'s first collection of poems. Her work appears in *Journal of Kentucky Studies*.

Laurie Clewett is glad to be writing poems again after a ten-year drought. She lives in her hometown of Lexington, Kentucky.

Samantha Cole is a poet from Beattyville, Kentucky. She hopes the love she feels for the mountains ring true in her words.

SuzAnne C. Cole writes in the Texas Hill Country. Both a juried and featured poet for Houston Poetry Fest, she's won a Japanese haiku contest.

Roger Craik is the author of three books of poetry. He lives in Ashtabula, Ohio.

Dean Crawford is a native of Louisville, and a graduate of the University of Kentucky. He is married with two grown children and retired from state government.

Philip Dacey, a three-time Pushcart Prize winner, has written entire collections of poems about Gerard Manley Hopkins, Thomas Eakins, and New York City.

Adam Day is the recipient of a 2010 Poetry Society of America Chapbook Fellowship for *Badger, Apocrypha*.

Sonja de Vries is a Kentucky-born writer and activist living on a farm outside Louisville. She is the author of *Planting A Garden In Baghdad*.

Mark DeCarteret served as the seventh Poet Laureate of Portsmouth, New Hampshire from 2009–2011. You can check out his Postcard Project at pplp.org.

Albert DeGenova has four poetry collections to his credit. He is the editor/publisher of the literary/arts magazine *After Hours*. He lives in Oak Park, Illinois.

Joanie DiMartino is the author of *Strange Girls* (Little Red Tree Publishing) and *Licking the Spoon* (Finishing Line Press), and past winner of the Betty Gabehart Award for Poetry.

Lynnell Edwards' most recent collection of poetry is *Covet* (Red Hen Press, 2011). She is Associate Professor of English at Spalding University.

Alan Elyshevitz is from East Norriton, Pennsylvania. His poetry has appeared recently in *The Broken Plate*, *U.S. 1 Worksheets*, and *Wilderness House Literary Review*.

Nettie Farris teaches writing at the University of Louisville and Indiana University Southeast. She has published in *The Journal of Kentucky Studies*, *Appalachian Heritage*, and *The Louisville Review*.

Nancy Fierstien is a Dripping Springs, Texas writer actively involved with the Austin Poetry Society. She hosts a monthly venue for poets and songwriters.

Anthony Fife is a professor of English and lives in Yellow Springs, Ohio, with his partner, fiction writer Lauren Shows, and their daughter Lucy.

Ken Fifer has published four collections of poetry, and his poems have appeared in *Barrow Street, The Wolf* (UK), *Ploughshares,* and many other journals.

Maureen Tolman Flannery's recent books include *Destiny Whispers to the Beloved* and *Ancestors in the Landscape.* Her poems have appeared in fifty anthologies and over a hundred literary reviews.

Gerald Fleming's most recent books of poetry are *Swimmer Climbing onto Shore* (Sixteen Rivers Press) and *Night of Pure Breathing: Prose Poems,* from Hanging Loose Press in Brooklyn.

Marguerite Floyd holds an MFA in Writing from Vermont College. Her books include *Everyone's Daughter* (poetry), *The African Brown-Headed Parrot* (non-fiction), and *The Parrot Reckonings* (humor).

Ruth Foley's work is appearing or forthcoming in *River Styx, Measure, The Ghazal Page,* and *Umbrella.* She is Associate Poetry Editor for *Cider Press Review.*

Anthony Frame, an exterminator from Toledo, Ohio, wrote *Paper Guillotines* (Imaginary Friend Press, 2010), has poems in lots of places. Learn more at anthony-frame.com.

Tom Frazier teaches English at University of the Cumberlands and recently read his work at Evening With the Poets at Hazard Community and Technical College.

Sarah Freligh is the author of *Sort of Gone* (2008). She has received poetry fellowships from the National Endowment for the Arts and the Saltonstall Foundation.

Wanda Fries teaches English at Somerset Community College. Her writing has appeared in various journals, including *Sojourners* and *The Michigan Quarterly Review*.

Joy Gaines-Friedler's poems are widely published. Her book, *Like Vapor* was published by Mayapple Press. Please visit joygainesfriedler.com. Yes, that is a real tiger.

Martha Gehringer is a teacher of writing in her 27th year as a member of the faculty of Transylvania University in Lexington, Kentucky.

Jane Gentry, Kentucky Poet Laureate 2007–2009 and English professor at the University of Kentucky, is the author of two poetry collections published by LSU Press.

Barry George's haiku and tanka have been widely published. He is the author of *Wrecking Ball and Other Urban Haiku*, from Accents Publishing.

Karen George has received grants from The Kentucky Foundation for Women and The Kentucky Arts Council. Her chapbook, *Into the Heartland*, is available from Finishing Line Press.

Kathleen Gerard's prose and poetry have been widely published as well as broadcast on National Public Radio (NPR).

Carmen Germain's poetry collection *These Things I Will Take with Me* was published by Cherry Grove. She lives in the Elwha river valley, Washington state.

Jo Going writes and paints her way around the circumpolar north. Most of her imagery is based in her life in the wilderness of interior Alaska.

Andrei Guruianu is the author of three collections of poetry and the memoir *Metal and Plum* (Mayapple Press, 2010). Most recent interest—digital photography.

279

Piotr Gwiazda is the author of two books, *James Merrill and W.H. Auden: Homosexuality and Poetic Influence* (Palgrave Macmillan, 2007) and *Gagarin Street Poems* (WWPH, 2005).

Colleen S. Harris is author of three books of poetry: *The Kentucky Vein* (Punkin House), *These Terrible Sacraments* (Bellowing Ark), and *God in My Throat: The Lilith Poems* (Bellowing Ark).

Matthew Haughton has published one chapbook, *Bee-coursing Box* (Accents Publishing). His work has appeared in many journals and magazines. Haughton lives in Lexington, Kentucky.

Petja Heinrich is the author of three poetry collections. She lives in Germany.

Kathleen Hensley = Hensley House (*Monolith Magazine*, *Abstract Series* drawing books, environmental sound recordings), Harvard writing graduate student, co-editor Hey Small Press!, seamstress, runner, dreamer, firestarter.

Ruth Holzer is the author of two chapbooks. Her poetry has been published in various literary journals and has received nominations for the Pushcart Prize.

Paul Hostovsky's latest book of poems, *A Little in Love a Lot,* is available from Main Street Rag.

Rebecca Gayle Howell's poems and translations appear in such publications as *Ninth Letter*, *Massachusetts Review*, *Ecotone*, *Indiana Review*, *Hayden's Ferry Review*, and *Poetry Daily*.

Charlie Hughes is the author of two books of poetry and he is the owner of Wind Publishing.

Tom C. Hunley is the author of three full-length poetry collections, four chapbooks and two books of prose about poetry.

Elizabeth Iannaci holds an MFA in Poetry, lives in Los Angeles, remembers when there really were orange groves, and shares birthdays with Red China and Julie Andrews.

Darren Jackson is the Editor of *Grist: The Journal for Writers*. His work has appeared in *Smartish Pace*, *Iron Horse*, *Cimarron Review* and other journals.

Libby Falk Jones is Professor of English at Berea College. Her poems have been published in journals and anthologies and in her chapbook, *Above the Eastern Treetops, Blue* (Finishing Line Press, 2010).

Marilyn Kallet is the author of 15 books, including *Packing Light: New and Selected Poems* (Black Widow Press, 2009). She directs the creative writing program at the University of Tennessee.

Lisa Kang is a frequent contributor to *Calliope* children's magazine. Her poetry has appeared in *GUD: Greatest Uncommon Denominator*, *The View From Here*, and *Earth's Daughters*.

J. Kates is a poet and translator. He is the author of *Metes and Bounds* (Accents Publishing, 2010).

Ruth Moon Kempher has operated Kings Estate Press in St. Augustine, Florida since 1994. The Press will soon issue her latest collection, a collaboration with Wayne Hogan.

Leatha Kendrick is author of three books of poetry, most recently *Second Opinion* (2008). Her poems appear widely in anthologies and journals. She teaches at the Carnegie Center in Lexington, KY.

Jen Kohan is a writer and writing teacher based in Minneapolis. Her poetry has appeared in *Audemus*, and creative nonfiction in *Break the Silence*.

Sari Krosinsky's first book, *god-chaser*, is forthcoming from CW Books. She edits *Fickle Muses*. She received an M.A. from the University of New Mexico.

Francis Krug is a dance instructor at Fred Astaire Dance Studios and currently lives in Indianapolis, Indiana. His life is writing and dancing.

Ellen LaFleche has worked as a journalist and women's health educator in Massachusetts. She has published poems in *Many Mountains Moving*, *Juked*, *Harpur Palate*, and *Alligator Juniper*.

Nana Lampton is the author of three volumes of poetry, most recently *Bloom on a Split Board* (Accents Publishing, 2011).

Peggy Landsman lives in South Florida where she swims in the warm Atlantic Ocean every chance she gets. She also writes. peggylandsman.com.

Ivan Landzhev is a Bulgarian poet and writer, a philosophy graduate from Sofia University. He has won several national poetry awards.

Caroline LeBlanc is a military family member and former Army Nurse. She leads *Writing For Your Life* © programs for soldiers, veterans, and their family members.

Carol Levin published two chapbooks and forthcoming full volume from Pecan Grove Press, 2012. She is Editorial Assistant at *Crab Creek Review*.

Gail Carson Levine is a children's book author. Her collection of humorous *This Is Just to Say* poems will be published by HarperCollins in 2012.

Richard Levine is the author of *A Language Full of Wars and Songs*, *Snapshots from a Battle*, and mostly recently *That Country's Soul* (Finishing Line Press, 2010).

The sole proprietor of **Jennifer Litt** Writing Services, Jennifer teaches writing at Saint John Fisher and Monroe Community Colleges in Rochester, New York.

Nicholas Liu's poems have appeared in *Mantis, Poetry Review* and elsewhere. His first book is *Versions from the English* (firstfruits, 2011). He lives in Singapore.

Joel Long writes from Salt Lake City. His books include *Knowing Time by Light* and *Winged Insects*.

JoAnn LoVerde-Dropp is the poetry workshop facilitator for The Georgia Writers' Association, and she teaches Poetry Memoir workshops in both Georgia and North Carolina.

Christina Lovin is the author of *What We Burned for Warmth* and *Little Fires*. Her work is supported by Kentucky Arts Council, Kentucky Foundation for Women, Elizabeth George Foundation.

Gregory Luce is the author of the chapbooks *Signs of Small Grace* (Pudding House Publications) and *Drinking Weather* (Finishing Line Press). He lives in Washington, DC.

George Ella Lyon's most recent poetry collection is *Back* (Wind, 2010). Visit her online at georgeellalyon.com.

Aimee Mackovic is the author of *A Sentenced Woman* (Finishing Line Press, 2007). Currently, she is an adjunct instructor for Keiser University and freelance writer.

Charlotte Mandel has published seven books of poetry, the most recent, *ROCK VEIN SKY*, from Midmarch Arts Press. Visit her at charlottemandel.com.

Arlene L. Mandell, a retired English professor, has published more than 500 poems, essays and short stories in newspapers and literary journals.

Jesse Manley earned his MFA in poetry from the University of New Orleans and is an editor emeritus of *Bayou Magazine* and *Ellipsis*.

Katie Manning is Editor-in-Chief of *Rougarou*, a doctoral fellow in English at UL-Lafayette, and a daily visitor to the nearby swamp.

Prairie L. Markussen lives and writes in Daegu, South Korea, where she teaches English. She received her MFA in Poetry from Roosevelt University in Chicago.

Chris Mattingly is the author of *Ad Hoc* and *A Light for Your Beacon,* both from Q Ave Press. He lives and works in Louisville, Kentucky.

Lori A. May is the author of four books, including *stains: early poems*. Visit her online at loriamay.com.

Born and raised in Eastern Kentucky, **Jay McCoy** now lives in Lexington. He is a member of Poezia writing group and often participates in local poetry readings.

Christopher McCurry usually writes poems about love, his cat, his neighborhood, and anything magical. He teaches and lives in Lexington, Kentucky with his girlfriend, Eloise.

John McKernan is now a retired comma herder. He lives— mostly—in West Virginia, where he edits *ABZ Press*. His most recent book is of selected poems, *Resurrection of the Dust*.

Ottawa writer **rob mclennan** is the author of over 20 books of poetry, fiction and non-fiction, and regularly posts reviews, essays, interviews and more at robmclennan.blogspot.com.

Karen McPherson is a poet, a translator of contemporary Quebec poetry and essays, and a professor of Francophone Studies at the University of Oregon.

Andrew Merton's first book of poetry will be released by Accents Publishing in 2012. He teaches writing at the University of New Hampshire.

Norman Minnick is the author of *To Taste the Water* and editor of *Between Water and Song: New Poets for the Twenty-First Century.*

Suchoon Mo is a former Korean Army lieutenant and a retired academic living in the semiarid part of Colorado. His poems and music compositions have appeared widely.

Trey Moody lives in Lincoln, Nebraska, and is the author of *Climate Reply* (New Michigan Press/DIAGRAM) and *Once Was a Weather* (Greying Ghost Press).

Larry W. Moore is a publisher (Broadstone Books) and gallery curator in Frankfort, Kentucky. Photographer, translator and reviewer, his poetry appears in the *Journal of Kentucky Studies* and others.

David Park Musella is an author, editor, and activist who originated in Buffalo, New York, and currently resides in Lexington, Kentucky.

Kristine Ong Muslim has poetry and prose appearing in hundreds of publications, including *Boston Review*, *Narrative Magazine*, *The Pedestal Magazine*, and *Southword*.

Constance Norgren is the author of the chapbook *Same Boat*, published by 5 Spice Press. She lives in Brooklyn with her family. She won first prize in the 2011 Split This Rock Poetry Contest.

Mary E. O'Dell is founder and president of Green River Writers, Inc. and has published several poetry collections. Her first novel, *The Sweet Letting Go*, was published by Turquoise Morning Press.

Andrea O'Rourke, a native of Croatia, lives in Atlanta, Georgia, where she paints abstracts and attends the New South Poetry Workshop at Georgia State University.

Elizabeth Oakes' most recent book of poems is *Mercy in the New World* (Wind, 2010). She lives in Bowling Green and Sedona, AZ.

Jeremy Dae Paden was born in Italy and raised in Latin America. He teaches Spanish at Transylvania University. He has poems here, there, and yon.

Joe Peacock's recent writings include a short story in *Trajectory* and a review of Pat Conroy's *My Reading Life* for *Southern Humanities Review.*

Richard Pearse's *Private Drives: Selected Poems 1969–2001,* is out, and his poems and stories have appeared in over thirty magazines. He lives in New York City.

Roger Pfingston is a retired teacher of English and photography. A new chapbook, *A Day Marked for Telling,* will be published in the fall of 2011 by Finishing Line Press.

Emilia Phillips is the 2010–2011 lead associate editor of *Blackbird.* Her poetry has appeared in *Copper Nickel, Indiana Review, Sycamore Review,* and elsewhere.

Kenneth Pobo has a new chapbook out from Thunderclap Press called *Closer Walks.* His work appears in *Word Riot, Stickman Review, Public Republic, 2River View,* and elsewhere.

Sheila Bucy Potter is the author of *Home Place and Other Poems,* published by Broadstone Books.

Melva Sue Priddy, a native Kentuckian, lives with her husband Gene Strode, who has helped provide a safe environment for writing.

Brett Eugene Ralph is the author of *Black Sabbatical* (Sarabande, 2009). The debut album by Brett Eugene Ralph's Kentucky Chrome Revue is available from Noise Pollution.

Peter Ramos' most recent collection of poetry is called *Please Do Not Feed the Ghost* (BlazeVOX Books, 2008).

Jerry Ratch has published 12 books of poetry, the novel *Wild Dreams of Reality*, and the memoir *A Body Divided*. See his website: jerryratch.com.

Mary Anne Reese is a poet and attorney in Cincinnati, Ohio. Her poetry chapbook is *Raised by Water* (Finishing Line Press).

Ken Rice is a Midwesterner (Michigan and Illinois) and social scientist whose poetry writing, those close to him say, is proof of a mid-life crisis.

Author of *Chinoiserie* (Ahsahta Press, 2012), **Karen Rigby** lives in Arizona. Her website is www.karenrigby.com.

Bobbi Dawn Rightmyer is a life-long resident of Harrodsburg, Kentucky who has been writing since age 11. She has been published in several magazines and newspapers.

Nick Ripatrazone is the author of *Oblations* (Gold Wake Press, 2011); his writing has also appeared in *Esquire, The Kenyon Review, Sou'wester* and *West Branch*.

Zack Rogow is the author, editor, or translator of eighteen books or plays. His sixth book of poems, *The Number Before Infinity,* was published by Scarlet Tanager Books.

Gabriele A. Rollé lives in an unfashionable part of Brooklyn, supporting herself and her reading habit with an office job in the financial services industry.

Rosemary Royston lives in northeast Georgia. Her poetry has been published in *Alehouse, The Comstock Review, Main Street Rag, Public Republic* and other journals.

Barbara Sabol has authored two chapbooks, *Original Ruse* and *The Distance Between Blues*. Her poetry has appeared widely. Barbara has an MFA from Spalding University.

Richard Schiffman is a poet and author of two biographies. His "Spiritual Poetry Portal" can be found at multiplex.isdna.org/poetry.htm.

Ada Jill Schneider directs "The Pleasure of Poetry" at the Somerset Public Library in Massachusetts. Her latest book is *Behind the Pictures I Hang* (Spinner Publications, 2007).

Staci R. Schoenfeld is an MFA candidate in poetry at Southern Illinois University. Her poems have been published in *Appalachian Heritage, Still,* and other fine journals.

Jan Seale's published work includes six books of poetry, two of which are *The Wonder Is* and *Valley Ark.* janseale.com.

Claudia Serea is a Romanian-born poet, and the author of two poetry collections: *Eternity's Orthography* (Finishing Line Press) and *To Part Is to Die a Little* (Červená Barva Press).

Jeanne Shannon lives in Albuquerque, New Mexico where she writes poetry and short fiction and conducts poetry workshops.

J.D. Smith's third collection of poetry, *Labor Day at Venice Beach*, is forthcoming in 2012. He periodically provides updates at jdsmithwriter.blogspot.com.

Frederick Smock is associate professor of English at Bellarmine University, and the author of five collections of poetry.

Paul Sohar, chemist for a living, poet for the soul, has nine books of translations and one of his own: *Homing Poems* (Iniquity Press, 2005).

Merry Speece has published a mixed-genre work, *Sisters Grimke Book of Days,* and two chapbooks of poetry. She lives in Ohio.

Affrilachian Poet and Cave Canem Fellow, **Bianca Spriggs**, is the author of *Kaffir Lily* and *How Swallowtails Become Dragons*. She lives in Lexington, Kentucky.

Christine Strevinsky is Polish-born and has been a mail inserter and an English teacher and a writer. A Katrina refugee, she now resides in Kentucky.

Karen Stromberg is a dedicated minimalist who favors the short poem, flash fiction and the 10-minute play.

A Cuban-born writer, **Dariel Suarez** is currently an MFA candidate at Boston University. His work has appeared in *SmokeLong Quarterly*, *Versal*, and *Midway Journal*.

David Sullivan's first book, *Strong-Armed Angels,* was published by Hummingbird Press. Two poems were read by Garrison Keillor on *The Writer's Almanac.*

Eric Scott Sutherland, author of *incommunicado*, lives in Lexington, Kentucky. He is the creator and host of the Holler Poets Series, a monthly celebration of literature and music.

Richard Taylor is a former Kentucky poet laureate and has authored books of poetry, fiction and non-fiction.

Jeanie Thompson directs The Alabama Writers' Forum and teaches in the Spalding University brief-residency MFA in Writing Program. Her latest book is *The Seasons Bear Us*.

Jessica Thompson lives and writes in a purple house in southern Indiana. Her poetry has appeared in numerous small press journals and magazines across the country.

Matthew Thorburn is the author of *Subject to Change* (New Issues, 2004) and *Every Possible Blue* (CW Books, forthcoming 2012).

Allison Thorpe's poem is from a manuscript she is developing based on the work of Georgia O'Keefe.

Cristina Trapani-Scott studied writing at Spalding University. Her poems have appeared in *Hip Mama, Public Republic* and *Sweet Lemons 2: International Writings with a Sicilian Accent.*

Organic fruit grower **Rosemerry Wahtola Trommer** lives in Southern Colorado. Three word mantra: I am learning. One word mantra: Adjust.

Wendy Vardaman (wendyvardaman.com) is the author of *Obstructed View* (Fireweed Press) and the co-editor and webmaster of *Verse Wisconsin* (versewisconsin.org).

Marian Veverka has spent most of her life on the shores of Lake Erie. She loves poetry, beaches and grandchildren.

James Vincent is the godfather of cash.

Georgia Wallace is the author of *The Coming Fall*, recently released by Finishing Line Press, and a previous chapbook, *My Father's Daughter* (Grex Press).

Thom Ward is the author of several books of poetry, most recently *Etcetera's Mistress* (Accents Publishing, 2011).

Burton D. Wasserman lives in New Rochelle, New York, and has published three books of poetry. He was nominated for the Pushcart Prize for 2010.

Chocolate Waters lives and writes in Manhattan. Her latest collection, *the woman who wouldn't shake hands* is now available from Poets Wear Prada.

Amy Watkins is co-editor and host of the weekly poetry podcast *Red Lion Square*. She lives in Florida with her husband and only child, Alice.

Lenore Weiss awaits two poetry collections to be published in 2011: *Tap Dancing on the Silverado Trail,* from Finishing Line Press, and *Mother and Other Love,* West End Press.

Judith Wiker is a confessional poet/songwriter, an artist with cross-genre appeal. *Children of Fire* is her most recent collection of poems.

John Sibley Williams' chapbooks include *A Pure River* (2010) and *Door, Door* and *The Art of Raining* (2011) and awards include a Pushcart nomination and the Heart Award.

Joe Willkins is the author of *The Mountain and the Fathers* and *Killing the Murnion Dogs*. He lives with his family on the north Iowa prairie.

Dylan Willoughby has recently received fellowships from Yaddo and The MacDowell Colony. Chester Creek Press published his chapbook *Dusk at St. Mark's*.

Keith S. Wilson is an Affrilachian Poet and Cave Canem Fellow living in Kentucky.

Nicholas YB Wong is the author of *Cities of Sameness* (Desperanto, forthcoming). He is currently a poetry editor for *THIS Literary Magazine* and a poetry reader for *Drunken Boat*.

Robert E. Wood teaches at Georgia Tech in Atlanta. His chapbook, *Gorizia Notebook,* was published by Finishing Line Press.

Marianne Worthington is co-founder and poetry editor of *Still: The Journal* and editor of the *Motif Anthology Series* from MotesBooks. She lives in Williamsburg, Kentucky.

Sheri L. Wright is the author of five books of poetry. Her work has appeared in numerous journals, including *Crucible* and *Earth's Daughters*.

Lisa Zimmerman's latest collection is *The Light at the Edge of Everything* (Anhinga Press, 2008). She's an assistant professor at the University of Northern Colorado.

Acknowledgments

"#1 of Philippa's Questions," Olivia V. Ambrogio, *The Herbal Network*

"A Blessing," Matthew Thorburn, *32 Poems*

"And," Kristine Ong Muslim, *Ex Cathedra Literary Magazine*

"Anniversary of the Death of a Child," Amy Watkins, *The Louisville Review*, Fall 2006

"Answers," Georgia Wallace, *The Coming Fall*

"At Jane's Dojo," Sari Krosinsky, *The Same*

"At Sea," Burton D. Wasserman, *Between the Totems of Labor and Love*, Daniel & Daniel, 2001

"At the Gate," Zack Rogow, *American Tanka*, 2006

"Autumn," Jeanne Shannon, *Luna: Myth and Mystery*

"Badger Eats," Adam Day, *Badger, Apocrypha*, Poetry Society of America

"Bread," Karen Rigby, *Savage Machinery*, Finishing Line Press, 2008

"Cross, how comfortable you are," John Sibley Williams, *Sleet Magazine*

"cycle," Mark DeCarteret, *Rolling Home Tour* blog site

"Directions," David Chorlton, *Brevities*

"Divorcing the Strong Man," Joanie DiMartino, *Strange Girls*, Little Red Tree Publishing, 2010

"Elegy for Lorri," Brett Eugene Ralph, *Black Sabbatical*, Sarabande Books, 2009

"fable," Mark DeCarteret, *Lilliput Review*

"Fe/Male," Libby Falk Jones, *Phoenix*, 1985; *Above the Eastern Treetops, Blue*

"Fragment from Zeno," J.D. Smith, *Anon*

"Further Shores," J.D. Smith, *Milk Money*

"His First Cry," Elizabeth Iannaci, *How Luminous the Wildflowers*, Tebot Bach Press

"I unwind the hose, send a light spray," Elizabeth Brennan, *HaikuPix Review*

"I Used To," Chocolate Waters, *Cedar Hill Review; Women's Glib Cartoon Calendar 1993*, Edited by Roz Warren

"Independence," Nancy Fierstien, *Inks Lake Ink*, Burnet (Texas) Cultural Arts Festival, 2007

"-ING," Nicholas YB Wong, *Poetry Super Highway*

"January," Brett Eugene Ralph, *27 Years*, White Fields Press, 1994

"Lighthouse," Karen Stromberg, *Hummingbird*

"Longing," Kate Angus, *Cellpoems*

"Love me," Claudia Serea, *Respuestas: The Neruda Project*

"Lust," Richard Levine, *Rattapallax*

"Magic," Nicholas Ripatrazone, *Eclectica*

"Match-Made," Dariel Suarez, *elimae*

"Metropolitan Diary," Richard Levine, *Rattapallax*

"Midwest Apocalypse," Mary Anne Reese, *Raised by Water*, Finishing Line Press, 2011

"Nicolae and Elena Ceausescu," Peggy Landsman, *Contemporary Literary Horizon*

"No More," Sherry Chandler, *Weaving a New Eden*

"Note to an Ex," Aimee Mackovic, *A Sentenced Woman*, Finishing Line Press

"On the Way Home from Lexington to Frankfort via Leestown Road," Staci R. Schoenfeld, *Still: The Journal*

"Pear," Kristine Ong Muslim, *Ginosko Literary Journal*

"Poem Found on Nicholasville Road," Charlie Hughes, *Body and Blood*, Wind Publications, 2010

"Puddle," Richard Levine, *New York Times*

"Remembering the Original," Trey Moody, *Climate Reply*, New Michigan Press, 2010

"Robin in the Rafters," Richard M. Berlin, *Psychiatric Times*

"Separate sections in Mexican cemeteries," Alex Cigale, *Four and Twenty*

"Shut Up!," Suchoon Mo, *Hobo Camp Review*

"Silhouette," Peggy Landsman, *Alba*

"Statement of a Refugee from Babel," J. Kates, *Cyphers*

"Sunflower River Road," Joe Willkins, *Tar River Poetry*

"The Art of Giving," Kathleen Gerard, *Feile-Festa*

"The Collapse," Lenore Weiss, *California Quarterly*

"The Dead," Piotr Gwiazda, *Gagarin Street: Poems*, Washington Writers' Publishing House, 2005

"The Discovery of Father Francisco Javier Saeta's Remains," David Chorlton, *Brevities*

"The Dying," Joe Peacock, Literary LEO's writing contest, 2005

"The Paraplegic's Paradox," Nancy Fierstien, *Di-verse-City Anthology*, Austin International Poetry Festival

"The Quietest Thing," Ellen LaFleche, *Ovarian*, Dallas Poets Community, 2011

"The Road Home," Roger Pfingston, *Poetry Midwest*

"The wonder is," Jan Seale, *The Wonder Is*, Panther Creek Press, 2005

"The Wrist," J. Kates, *The Bellingham Review*

"The Zen of Mountain Driving," Christina Lovin, *New Southerner*

"Theosophy," Kate Angus, *Cellpoems*

"Thirst," Marilyn Kallet, *In the Great Night*, Ithaca House, 1981

"This small poem," Anthony Frame, *Versal*

"Thumb," Philip Dacey, *Mosquito Operas: New and Selected Short Poems*, Rain Mountain Press, 2010

"Time Passing," Kate Angus, *Cellpoems*

"titleless," Mark DeCarteret , *3rd bed*

"To An Unfallen Leaf (Northern Pin Oak)," Dylan Willoughby, *litrasfalsas*

"Today I Threw Out Your Toothbrush," Jesse Manley, *The Rio Grande Review*

"Violin," Merry Speece, *Detail from an American Landscape*, Bits Press, 1979

"Visit to a Winery," Sheila Bucy Potter, *Home Place and Other Poems*, Broadstone Books, 2003

"Watercolor," Sari Krosinsky, *abqARTS*

"Winter Harvest," Nettie Farris, *The Journal of Kentucky Studies*

"Young Veteran," Colleen S. Harris, *These Terrible Sacraments: poems*, Bellowing Ark Press, 2010

A Note from the Editor

My deep gratitude to all poets who submitted work for this anthology and to all who share the love of the short poem.

Special thanks to Accents Publishing interns Chris McCurry, Jackson Coffer and Francis Krug for their dedication and hard work.

About the Editor

Katerina Stoykova-Klemer is the author of two full-length poetry books and a chapbook. She hosts a weekly literary radio show called *Accents*.

About This Book

Every poem in *Bigger Than They Appear* consists of no more than 50 words, including the title.

Chapooks by Accents Publishing

Full-Length World Poetry Series